Leave It Raw

poems by

Shakira Croce

Finishing Line Press
Georgetown, Kentucky

Leave It Raw

Copyright © 2020 by Shakira Croce
ISBN 978-1-64662-265-8 First Edition
All rights reserved under International and Pan-American Copyright Conventions. No part of this book may be reproduced in any manner whatsoever without written permission from the publisher, except in the case of brief quotations embodied in critical articles and reviews.

ACKNOWLEDGMENTS

Grateful acknowledgment is made to the following publications in which some of these poems first appeared:

Ducts: "Blue Ridge Mountain Runaway," "Searchlight"
New Ohio Review: "Venus Out on the Town"
HIV Here & Now: "Our Song"
Red River Review: "A Cry for a Witness"
pioneertown: "Broadcasting the Search for the Missing"
Permafrost Magazine: "Pilgrimage"
Pilgrimage Press: "Cycle"

Publisher: Leah Maines
Editor: Christen Kincaid
Cover Art and Design: Warren Croce, www.warrencroce.com
Author Photo: Gaya Feldheim Schorr

Order online: www.finishinglinepress.com
also available on amazon.com

Author inquiries and mail orders:
Finishing Line Press
P. O. Box 1626
Georgetown, Kentucky 40324
U. S. A.

Table of Contents

Blue Ridge Mountain Runaway 1

The Remains 2

Homecoming 4

Commuter's Pastoral 6

Searchlight 7

Venus Out on the Town 8

Our Song 10

Departure 11

A Cry for a Witness 13

Before You Press That Button 14

I Got Cable 15

Broadcasting the Search for the Missing 16

I've Left Time for Questions at the End 18

Old Love Notes 19

Last Movement 20

On a Familiar Ride 21

Pilgrimage 23

Break from the Headlines 24

Our Hands 25

Hopes and Dreams 26

Misdiagnosis 27

Prelude 28

Second Honeymoon 29

Cycle 30

For Shawn and Julian

Blue Ridge Mountain Runaway

High cries broke
from that salt-beaded neck
above splintered hands
dangling on strings.
Now rest hushed in moonshine
between bar lines
as lead begins to drip.
We escaped on the trail of rhapsody
to the crossroads of flattened steps
until the air had a bite
facing an Aeolian hall.
You reworked the elements
and shot into a deep heavy dazzle
slapping guts, beating petticoats to pop
and shed away to flaps.
And mine fell in the middle of waves
of underwire domes weighted in their seats,
hissing what good will come since we began with that form.
But as you bend
over me, my arms lift up and open,
as if none of us have ever done this before.

The Remains

With a pink sundress on a hazy August afternoon,
she waves him over to what's left of her porch.
Already looking her way through fireflies
starting to blink between sprinklers,
he jogs to her hopelessly
rubbing sunscreen on his burnt chest.
"Would you help me pick through this?"
She motions to cardboard boxes holding the remains
of yesterday's fire, pieces of china, her miniature collection,
photo albums, notebooks buried in dark gunk.
She wants him to tell her they can't be saved.
Her mother's sugar bowl, a white cat,
hasn't been found.
The wall by the corner cupboard went down first.
"It could have been worse,"
he says scratching soot off a porcelain doll, trying not to look
at her nipples lightly covered in cotton,
which wouldn't have surprised the parents on their street
of Confederate flags who whispered
about her black fingernails and mesh covering too much cleavage.
Before graduation, they'd talk into the night about moving to the capital,
made to live closely, even room together, taking turns
making dinner, mixing their colors and whites.
On the train home one day, a careless passenger
might push her nylon thighs into him.
Instead, they found work in town and settled at home,
wondering how the fire could have started,
until she changes the subject to their childhood.

He gave her his red balloon once
on her 5th birthday when her purple one flew
out the window,
but as soon as she took hold of the string
a gust of wind ripped it out of her hand and up into the sky.
It was the first time the two of them, after a pause,
stopped and looked deep and breathless into each other's eyes
and laughed.

Homecoming

It's about finding
the space
to bring out what's already
inside you.

Half-listening to the teacher,
she clenches bubblegum between her teeth,
removing it discreetly to study
their imprint on the fleshy pink.

Spit from the back row, likely from the same
hard-on that pressed against her yesterday,
she tries to ignore chicklets stuck in her hair,
focusing on the clock.

Winter light strains
down through the clouds,
signaling their release.
She locks and relocks her stall,

hurrying to change.
Their coach was wary
of the "community's reaction,"
but on her second year of tryouts

she made the team
and helped two friends make the cut
by reminding them to smile
from the bottom of the pyramid.

King and Queen
walk down the 50-yard line,
but she feels the arena of eyes
still on her.

From parade rest
the band snaps up
stepping into formation
to the beat of the snare.

And for a moment she is lost
to the crowd in a mass of uniforms
seen as one body of color
marching off the great field together.

Commuter's Pastoral

Defiance and freedom
marked the face of the aging man,
wiry mustache and cracked cheeks above
a lifted chin
as if weathered
from desert gusts and
afternoon sun beating through
a wide-brimmed hat.
His eyes held a history
of searching for prey or predators,
or perhaps just imagining
what his great-grandfather was like
and wondering what kind of space
contained the lives of his ancestors.
Was it just nothing but tumbleweed
between their fire and the next
and only a few bits to show for all
that time spent straddling horses?
But now there is no beast
against him and the rail
in the rush hour train
stalled before reaching the end of the line.

Searchlight

turning madly, mutely with 120 volts
fastened to ground the coy bonnet fidgets
streaming them lucidly to fortune and targets

they plunge deeper into foreign territory,
with fraying bootstraps inching into blackness digging
hastily before history remembers them ghosts

others, entrenched together chins wet with sludge
firing in a faraway land, a final moan
faces blown right down to the bone

a seven-year-old girl with a six-week-old scar asks:
why do they sing "and many more"?
with black-and-blue eyes on her birthday

let's change the subject to the translation
of the Blockbuster, to think it's already bringing in millions
how many billions more could be made?

everyone must find out about it
flashy promos for the biggest stars
there should be signs in lights

but how do you penetrate
the dark between naked maple's limbs
waiting to be coated in ice?

Venus Out on the Town

Yes, you may buy me
A drink

It has been a long week for me too
At work trading, you said?

No, you haven't had much?
Experience in social enterprise

Isn't it great we live in a country
Where you and your partners can pull such fine bootstraps

One of the brightest in the night, yes
I've been told I have a nice smile among other things

Your lines show in a few more years
Your advances will be harmless, cute even

Thank you for the champagne
What did you say your name was?

You were telling me something
About your problem of being unable

To find a good dry cleaner for your white button-downs
Yes, I'll have another

About your travels in Italy, did you see the naked Sabine
Captured in marble by so many chiseled arms

As she reaches above her alabaster
Gasp into the open air?

You were telling me something
She was much younger anyway

She told you it was over, you drink too much
No wonder you can't get it up

Sorry,
That was a cheap shot

I don't know why
I can be so defensive

Never mind, you were telling me something
I feel like it involved pills or dollars

And seeking counsel
Of course you had no idea

Excuse me, I don't mean to leave now
When we've just met and you've bought me

So many drinks
It's just that the French student across from us

I've been eying
With the carnation lips

And bud over his heart
Has just gone to smoke

And I wonder
What I'm missing

Maybe because there's something about this
Time of night ebbing like the foam on the sea

Our Song

Empty cars held us
in the pale grey turning
to square lights of the city.
The ambulance driver steps out to smoke,
tapping ashes on Park Avenue.
It came from Desert Storm,
and you keep it still stamped,
colors faded and oblivious
lying next to a half-empty pill box.
You choose the music tonight.
It's as simple as offering protection
from a line on the rise
in another CDC report failing to remind us
it's no longer a death sentence.
Sometimes we can forget it all:
put our song on repeat and dance
swinging arms around each other,
hearts beating wildly.
There's a greater communication
in that movement of the hip,
straighter than a needle
and wider than a lover's exhale
to reach the need.

Departure

She hurries from under
cranes hanging in the sky

anticipating the construction of the 29th floor
while the afternoon rush crawls down the avenue.

Windows hold scenes of silver, gold,
and mannequins dressed to the nines.

Finding nothing of interest to buy,
she stops at the shop advertising a new scent

selecting the tester of evergreen and vanilla
and letting the beads absorb on the curve of her neck.

Snow boots and oversized coats shiver together
as clouds of strangers' breath mingle

twirling and embracing
before dissipating into the twilight air.

Her bus arrives, and she sits
opposite a man who looks just like the actor

who played that famous deaf pianist,
or at least who has the same

beard, dark features she mused,
marveling at the light blue of his eyes.

She caught and held
his gaze, with the tenderness and strength

of knowing that this would be the extent
of their intimate moments,

unlike the wrinkled and swollen hand that reached
and prodded up her skirt last week,

though there were just as many people around them
holding the weight of unwrapped gifts.

She turns away, fixating on her nails,
remembering that though she felt

his hand on the inside of her thigh,
it did not feel like her body.

Looking back to the man,
she was surprised that he still held her face,

irises caressing her lips, ears, cheeks.
Their eyes met another time,

oblivious that she was being swept
out with the others at her stop.

In the cold she watches him searching
her seat, the exit, then out the window

as the bus pulls away.
She lingers with the exhaust fumes

before returning home feeling
somehow less alone than when she rose that morning.

A Cry for a Witness

Please pry me away
from my precious pages,

sticking together in their obsession
with vertigo titles and numbered typeface
fusing more kryptonite sighs.

I don't want to be inside
another cover's chubby nude.

Bag up these moldy rags
before skin fades to cheap newspaper.

Make my tongue roll
with another extremity,
and shred its naïve point.

Leave on these stained sheets
bread crusts, oil-cured olive pits,
and round stemmed crystals spotted purple.

Shatter my blank scribbled squares,
and pour me out
into the un-mirrored glass
that I can never see.

Before the rose stems grow soft and stink,

press between my bones fiercely
up against moments of eternity.

Before You Press That Button

Do you ever check the weather in another state
Or another hemisphere?
Is it getting cold there?
The first question from my aunt
Calling from across the Atlantic on a spotty connection
The news reports
He never had many friends and struggled with
Bad skin
Those closest to him called it the source of his insecurity
Early signs he would be lured by extremists
He became a master of universal coding
Sharing encryptions on social media
The investigation concluded to put him on a watch list
Taxpayer dollars steadily shuffled
Out of the arts to national security
Wait—
Before you press that button, I dare you to learn
To say: *Kiss me again*
Two falling stars that collide
Within the confines of the sky make no sound
But they have each other
In another language
There's a trigger way back
Next to the corner of the brain that flows
Into personal accounts that prove your theories
When sharing whiskey with friends
Not unlike the Biennale
Each structure holding a brilliant mind from their own world
Across the canal, a cellist
Reaches the double bar line of the third movement
The lift of her bow coming off the neck
Barely a reflection in the green-grey ripples
A full breath exhales into the final whole note
And sends a low hum across the sinking city
Reverberating in the frames that hold the wonders of each country

I Got Cable

Well I finally caved,
because I saw how good it was
on that big bed
that wasn't mine
on a floor
high up past where your ears pop.
The company paid for the room
and everything really.
So when I got back home,
I got cable
to better hole up
and nest and maybe fix
the cracks in the windows,
or invest in something solid like
an oak table that fits beneath the sill.
There's my hawk.
You can get a better look.
Leave the door unlocked;
see her claws clench in flight above my shutters.

Broadcasting	**the Search**	**for the Missing**
"If all we have is to sell we'll have no return"	time we can't	put money on him
He ends the call	at Terminal 1	hovering above the runway
far from tire swings	circled by pines	and honeysuckle
Back to the news in a dangerous attempt	Live a 31-year-old	from the Blue Hole believed to be
unable to undo the straps	wrapped around himself	
says the report	from the elevated screen	above waiting passengers
Delays as usual	and people	flooding the gates
He loosens his tie	watching the wings far from deep strokes	of the Last Judgment
Boarding another urgent ring	the final departure vibrates his pocket	unanswered
Without a witness	He was last seen here	There has been no body found

In the diagonal jet   teeth grind   eyes squint shut
                             and settle

And sometime   during the flight   amid the clouds

without reception
                             he drifts
                                                      back to ground

considering

The Skydiver

                    looking up now

                                              together with
                                              hardened sand

                    at beams of light streaming

                                              from 600 feet down

I've Left Time for Questions at the End

The problem is there still hasn't been
enough research
focused on the pipeline for girls
from foster care to incarceration.

We'll review one such case
beginning with the record of extreme humiliation
she expressed following the Ring Pop proposal,
a feeling of entrapment by the red sugar diamond.

The severity of her reaction around this event
was likely the cause of why no social worker
noted her self-absorption and general lack of interest
and never investigated how bad things were at home.

The absence of familial structure
soon led her to engage in high-risk behavior,
which was reinforced by her sexual partner
who was in and out of correctional facilities.

Undocumented violence and untreated trauma
(let's call it a gap in care)
around the trouble of being unable
to navigate multiple systems.

The subject is now serving
a three-year sentence in state prison
and suffers from a reoccurring nightmare
she is already dead.

Old Love Notes

Washing down tonight
with bourbon like great-grandfather

after they buried great-grandmother and the kids
moved north with families of their own,

the duo strums away in G,
resting after the bridge.

It's been years since I never became
the famous pianist my parents said I'd be.

Singing the refrain, glass clinks against the speaker
managing not to break this time.

I don't play often now or go out on the fire
escape anymore, remaining in scrolling

through feeds and down status updates.
There's a web of possibilities to plan one's last words:

Limit and direct your characters @SomeoneWellLiked,
and you'll go viral, runner-up to immortal

unlike the letters and cards I saved
to be lost one day, forgotten in a box

under my bed. Closing windows, I'm left with how
it might have been if I ever saw you again.

We would have surely hiked together
to the top of a great green mountain

snapping and sharing beautiful
pictures before the descent.

Last Movement

Remember the night we met
playing with wine, callous fingers
walking down the neck keeping time
to wails from the sax?
I didn't keep it a secret
that just a few years before I was young enough
to spend hours reaching up for honeysuckle
flowers peeking through the playground fence
to pluck and pinch them, pulling out their insides
and tasting the bit of sweetness at the tip.
The last year in the schoolyard,
they announced he found himself somehow
right between the mother bear and her cub.
The same year as the Chianti we sipped that night
I told you, and you took my number anyway.
On the last day of class all of us picked caterpillars
near the tree line to take home,
but after carrying mine through the tiled halls,
I snuck back out and let him go.
Riding with you in the cut grass
and hills of the winding country,
I wonder if anyone passing before us thought
to look back and save the box turtle
while his head hovered over the white line,
testing the road he intended to cross.

On a Familiar Ride

We entered Union to take a familiar ride,
and still we missed our stop.

Were we too busy averting our eyes
from paint-splattered jeans, greasy belts,

and gold-ringed wrists lining the rail?
Diesel mixed with Chanel made us tear-up.

Has it been so long since
our soles clacked on white marble

between rows of heels and ties
while Air played from the organ?

Herald came too soon
with a plague of plastic cups.

We squeezed in, cringing, waiting
for bodies to enter before the closing door.

Fishnets pressed against our pole,
and we wondered if it was midnight.

When I used to sing,
my teacher said my head should feel

like the dome of a church, but I was busy dreaming
of the long train I always wanted.

Ready to cross the East River, we studied
magnified black lungs and red-patched feet above us

with a number claiming to have the cure.
Beggars and preteens stumbled down the aisle freely

slinging their legs around the bars and shaking coins.
They pushed us between gum stuck on the seat.

How strange it was, as we glided between the others
we didn't even notice that we were walking

arm in arm above the bones of priests,
their names and dates smoothed with steps and faded.

Above ground we were almost home
where seagulls shift their weight in anticipation on the posts

as if they saw our rides were limited.

Even though we knew the sound of wheels
like running water, our eyes closed and heads nodded

limbs hanging heavily entwined.
We had the same dream then

we found out later
of leaving the ceremony with cheers and confetti,

and the ride took us along
to the end of the line without us knowing

in the empty car together.

Pilgrimage

We can make up time in the air,
the captain explained,
or at least that's what I understood
between the fuzzy intercom and
broken English,
not mentioning we'd lose
six hours crossing the Atlantic.
They say animals have a different
internal clock, without feeling
passing weeks and years.
Yet the butterfly with a tear
across her right wing
returns at noon each day
to that same turn in the road,
darting between rosemary and dandelions drying
in the honeyed weeds.
The sense of smell is the strongest
for us all to find food, a partner.
Flowers waiting to procreate on a cliff above the sea
bring me back to where I was born.
After spending a lifetime thousands of miles away
that simple power lets me know my home
is not where I live
but a long climb up from Roman rocks and ruins
to the stuff springing from
uncut earth.

Break from the Headlines

Leaving *Time* on the end table,
the mother went out with the neighborhood
to watch them bring down the oaks.
Strings from the block party
still clung to their limbs,
winter morning light giving
their naked dark brown a faint purple glow.
Someone on the street called-in the professionals,
who roped each one to the ground, saying
"There's no way to know how long
some have been there standing, already dead,
even more dangerous than the living."
Readying the blade, they struck quickly.
Bark splattered toward the others leaning
back with the weight of their bodies,
until metal hit the core.
Without a pause, they cut in deeper, when
louder than a gunshot, the first fell.
The next one, younger, dropped faster.
Too many to count splintered
and collapsed down the pavement like thunder.
Then—a hush—save
for the toddler, who no one heard had been wailing.
It was then the mother realized
a tear had broken from her lower
lashes, running
to rest on her cheek.
She had been out there with the others in the cold
and was too numb to notice.

Our Hands

I like receiving letters.
    You said once
    when you were young enough to be saved.
I believe my intentions were pure,
and I just wanted a friend,
though attention from the opposite
sex might have interested me.
Neither one of us would ever be
handsome, and I think we knew that then.
But I would become almost fluent
in a foreign language and listen
to piano concertos for four hands.
And you would be gone before
I found a clump of tissue clinging
softly above my heart.
I'm left scrolling down
your timeline searching for hints
of what we might have become
if there was no epidemic.
    Yesterday I could still remember
    something you wrote.
Our fingers nearly touching, picking at the bedsheets.
I never saw you die.

Hopes and Dreams

Her mother said she could have
been a famous artist,
but her subjects weren't relatable enough:

Six-foot-tall portraits of autumn leaves
sequentially fading in red, orange, brown
silhouettes obscured by earth,

and lately a series of eggs
in varying stages
of being swallowed by the hot, wet night.

Top galleries took notice,
but she priced everything
outrageously high and didn't have a website.

When she did show her paintings,
she selected those that appeared to be blank,
white-yellow veins of the maple barely distinguishable.

The viewer would really have to struggle
to be able to make out a blade or the delicate
texture of the yolk.

Eventually, she began a highly-celebrated career
in graphic design, sending canvases to the basement.
Children were always part of her plan, and she had several,

one of whom unsuccessfully attempted
to send her paintings to be nationally archived
the year following the funeral.

He was told he needed to put more time
into documenting dates, but his son was growing,
and he was responsible for finding somewhere to move
with enough space for crawling.

Misdiagnosis

Looking up from his notes,
the speaker raises a pencil as if to signal
the final chord of a symphony.
He's just finished a horror story
of a mother who died
after the system failed to detect
the underlying symptoms
behind her questions,
particularly around pain
and all the possible side effects
of their mismanagement.
Most cases of aching bones
are buried by a pattern
of chronic conditions and a family history
filed at a health center in the Bronx
or another high-risk neighborhood.
The specialist never pulled those records and
never tallied all those lost,
despite the paperwork
and lives devoted to preparations
for rapidly filling prescriptions.

Prelude

My voice changed, softened
upon the first view of that
beginning of a human. Sparks
from the part of the mind that lights when
recognizing the scent of late-summer
sea wheat. Feet dash across my split
abdominal wall as a chain of ants works its way
along the oak's trunk. I grasp your forearm
while the probe circles beneath him, trying to relax with
the safety of knowing these movements are protected
by layers of tissue. How long will it be before the colony
no longer needs that old bark and abandons their trail?
Seasons alternate, and blades make their way up
through concrete, sure as the small
steps soon to echo through our room.
At the back of an antique store we find
the same creamer my grandmother used.
My son might hold wonder for it like I did growing-up
confiding in its round glassy figure, or at least I can
house it on the bottom of the china cabinet—
save it from a quiet crumble.

Second Honeymoon

Last night I don't know why
we were fighting.
I think you felt like
everything was on your shoulders.

It's not the season for growing.
Pairs of raccoons drop tiny
speckled eggs and lap only
half the yoke.

Before we sink
back down into this soft grass,
let's take a trip.
JCPenney is going out of business.

Pick what our future granddaughter
will need, what we could have used
not long ago, pulling back the pups
barking at the swans.

Spend a full day scavenging
strip malls and thrift shops for a deal.
We can argue over directions and come out
with plastic play things and whiskey glasses.

It's time to plan
a break from working our way
up, shift scenery, and
rest our limbs from the climb.

Cycle

Motherhood reaches out
from the periphery, inaudible.
As a rush of feathers
signals the flock
plunging toward the tree line
of pines puncturing the biting sky.
They stand stiff, expectant of ice that will
edge along their needles and curves
of the great lake. She rocks
in my memory, in the corner
of the bar, guiding my fingers
through strands she gave me.
We weave the most incredible plait
and leave it raw,
unsewn straw running across tile.
A desire to want to produce
my own little girl before she's gone
grows, as the dried palm now
hangs in my closet, coiled around
old boxes of newspapers.
We shove them further back to clear
space for baby things.

Shakira Croce is a writer living in Brooklyn, New York. Croce's poetry translations have appeared in *Babel* magazine, and her poetry has been featured in several literary magazines and journals, including the *New Ohio Review, Pilgrimage Press, HIV Here & Now, Transactions, Ducts, pioneertown, Permafrost Magazine,* and *Shark Reef*. She was a featured reader in the Boundless Tales Reading Series, and she was a finalist in the Linda Flowers Literary Award competition.

Croce holds a Bachelor of Arts from Sarah Lawrence College and a Master's in Public Administration from Pace University. Born in Geneva, New York in 1987, she grew up in Gainesville, Georgia and later studied in Florence, Italy. She currently works in New York City as Assistant Director of Communications and Public Relations at New York's largest Medicaid Special Needs Health Plan, Amida Care. She lives with her husband, bass player and composer, Shawn Lovato; son, Julian Croce Lovato; and cats, Topo and Teddy.

www.ingramcontent.com/pod-product-compliance
Lightning Source LLC
LaVergne TN
LVHW041507070426
835507LV00012B/1388